# Come Morning...

---

## Thalamus' Ink.

---

## PEGASUS BOOKS

ISBN  0-9673123-7-X

Comments about *Come Morning...* and requests for additional copies may be addressed to Thalamus' Ink., c/o Pegasus Books, P.O. Box 232642, Sacramento, California 95823, or you can send them via e-mail to marco@pegasusbooks.net

# Come Morning...

*This book is dedicated to: Mrs. Ethel "Honey" Parker*
*For her timeless friendship and support as well as*
*an infinity's worth of love*


*Honorable mention goes to my Invincibles:*
*Ronald and Jay Douglas, Denise Turner, Anne Schwerner,*
*Henry Moses, Barbara Crawley, Henry Foster,*
*Hugo Charity, Daniel McCrimons,*
*Sondra K. Wilson, Marcelus Toney*
*And Luther H. Stewart*


*&*


*Special thanks to Mr. Marcus McGee whose invaluable friendship*
*and advice helped to make this book a reality. Blessings*


*Thalamus' Ink.*

# Come Morning...

## Arousal

## Enlightenment

# Wisdom

## Ashes From Other Loves

*Sunrise Photo on Cover by: Robin Michelini*

# *Arousal*

*Eyes to Visualize
Hearts to feel the joys and pains
Souls to understand*

## *The Blue Print Alternative*

*Life is ever changing*
*And who would chose the straight road*
*Never to veer*
*Never to bend*
*Never to ese*
*Solely to extend*
*And I have crossed it many times*
*Perhaps to find my way*

## The Shaken Sonnet

*Imprisoned by her own perfection*
*A princess was poised on her pedestal*
*Which served her well in its distinction*
*From a world distant still*

*On she danced in a circle*
*Revolving as a circle does*
*Once touched her cheeks blushed purple*
*Now not as perfect as she once was*

*Was this princess the better for it*
*Pirouette now interrupted*
*Or could she just ignore it*
*For her steps were not corrupted*

*She rutted the rim of the circle's distance*
*And wondered just further than its existence*

## *First Love*

*Eye kissed away*
*The virgin tears*
*Which swelled*
*Post liquid wake*

*Eye held her closely*
*Eye even held her tenderly*
*And felt her tremble*
*Before our warmth had fled*

*It was then that she lifted her eyes*
*To find our hearts in paradise*
*With talons freed before the land*
*And then the earth was gone*

# *Encore*

*Here we lie gasping for air*
*Fingers still clasped within each others*
*Joined as if in prayer*

*The aftermath of loves compliance*
*With ruffled rhythms on satin floors*
*Disturbing only ecstasy's silence*
*Like rushing tides upon the seashores*

*Our moisture and sweet melon breaths*
*Laid this symphony to rest*
*Exposing the acapella we did sing*
*Stripped of all save the notes of spring*

*While far off in the distance*
*The full moon offered no resistance*
*And bade us to play again*

## Hot Fudge Sundae

*I remember spring
With the snow slowly ceding
To its warmth
Forming fertility's template
Of wetness that
Dripped and oozed and ran
All over the land*

*I remember spring
With howling winds
Now pampered breezes
Which barely blew the leaves off trees
Then holding nature's perfumes
Within it's breath
At least until our breathing resumed*

*I remember spring
With the hawks last shrill
Echoing in the valley
Not taps but reveille
Waking both bear and butterfly
Arousing all as far
As that hawk could see*

*I remember spring
With buds like colors bursting to create
Canvasses of fields and forestlands
Of skies so vibrant they dared hands
To reach to touch to explore
To leave the confines of a glove
Never to return anymore*

*I remember spring*
*With your daisy dukes and bikini bra*
*The first sight of your skin*
*After the winter's thaw*
*And wondered with such little attire*
*How could your body feel so cold*
*While my mind was on fire*

*Oh I remember spring!*

## Synergy

*Shadows cast their ladyfingers*
*Then grope for the grasses*
*Which tease the light's fringe*

*Oaken umbrellas entice breezes*
*Which nose through our clothes*
*Then tickles the skin*

*These sacred grounds*
*Are magic carpets*
*Upon which we do lay*

*Chirping birds*
*Serenade with music*
*Enticing emotions which we display*

*Perfumed scents*
*Saturates nostrils…*
*You breathe out, my breathing rests*

*Serene summer uninterrupted*
*Perfectly sculpted*
*Your head on my chest*

*Who would leave*
*This oasis*
*As perfect as Shakespeare's plays*

*I could wish for nothing more*
*Except my love*
*For you to stay*

*Shadows cast their ladyfingers*
*Then grope for the grasses*
*Which tease the light's fringe*

*Oaken umbrellas entice breezes*
*You breathe out*
*And I breathe in*

## The Morning After

*I felt the impression*
*In ruffled sheets*
*Which you wove upon my bed*

*I felt the impression*
*Which you engraved upon my heart*
*And retraced with fingertips*
*This place where love began*

*Listen to the walls*
*Replaying all of our laughter*
*Or is*
*My heart amplified*

# Typo

*I would rather live my life*
*Than cling to these keys*
*As if they lived*

*For here the quested venture*
*Breathes only in retrospect*
*The gifted harvest*
*That Monday morning's cerebrations reap*

*From there to task*
*Contradictions exist*
*And so I sit*
*Tic, tick, tic, tick, tic, tick….*

# *Enlightenment*

*Life is like a snake
With so many twists and turns
And sharp fangs to shake*

## Etiology of a Flaw

*Should we not lament our heroes*
*Thorny spires these pinnacles*
*With so little room to build a foundation*
*Perhaps the basis*
*Of both our dooms*
*Errant thinking of a nation*

*Gargoyles guard*
*Or faith's foundations*
*To keep bad omens at bay*
*Or perhaps they started from inside*
*And rose to the rooftops to hide*
*But couldn't get away*

# The Circle's Destiny

*Yesterday intrudes upon each morn*
*As you arrive in springtime mists*
*Touching without being held*
*And only captured my sculpted worship*
*Until the sun summons its poise*
*To pilot my senses through*

*Chosen by dreams before day's eve*
*I have run a marathon of memories*
*To seek and fix some flaw in time*
*Or determine the purpose of our course*
*And then to set it straight*
*My mind seems destined to return*
*To mornings and mists*
*From which it still burns*

*Once expectant – now exhausted*
*Empty shell of a soul long plagued*
*Portraying the captor and its prisoner*
*Portraying the prisoner and its warden*
*With neither crime nor sentence known*
*I arise on the cusp of dawn*
*To see you appear in these misty morns*
*Then vanish in daylight's radiance*
*While I round the rind of the insane*
*Searching for the period*

## *Traces*

*Raindrops fill my window*
*Like the pearls of sweat*
*That form when lovers tango*
*Steps too quick to trace*
*Until that closing door*
*Sealed your goodbye*

*Reruns frame my mind*
*Your kisses are engraved upon my heart*
*And kindled a hunger that only addicts know*
*For each day you were life's purpose and*
*Distrusting the promise of tomorrow*
*Life would only start again once you did appear*

*Today my voice betrayed my heart*
*For it was my heart that needed volume*
*To reflect your best in me*
*I request your laughter and your protests*
*I demand your insistence and your nudging*
*Show that tenor to the door*

*Now raindrops fill my window*
*And dissolve your silhouette*
*As you race to meet the darkness*
*There's nothing left to subdue*
*The echoes and chills*
*That now fill this unfurnished mind*

*If you were not my heart or I yours*
*Then this death has found its rightful place*
*And let's set a stone upon it*

*But if a candle's flame exists*
*Darkness may surround*
*Until its light arouses the dawn*

*If in finding and then*
*Faltering with love*
*Should we not by reason*
*Seek the food to sustain it*
*Or the remedy to soothe its pain*
*Or the cement to seal its foundation*

*You are the candle's flame*
*And I shall await the morning*
*I hope that my part of your heart*
*Will listen to this plea*
*And trace the embers of my thoughts*
*Right here – back to me*

# Cackle 911

*From birds to missiles*
*Aimed at an ideal*
*To vaporize the paragons*
*The one hundred and ten*
*Reduced to twisted steel*
*With suffocating dust*
*Reigning upon the assassinated*
*The scorched the dismembered and the macerated*
*While the screen*
*Masked the pungent odor of gangrene*
*Fresh ghosts innocent and yet*
*Captured within deaths net*

*And others ran and stumbled*
*And others cried and retreated*
*While others ran head first*
*Into Hell's fury*
*And gifted others with life*
*And proved that God*
*Had heart and hands*

*Others waited and clenched their breasts*
*As each fallen story increased*
*The pain upon my chest*
*Until the floors*
*Each and ever one*
*Were reduced to none*
*And yet the sun will rise*
*Even in the face of this demise*

*While those who controlled the screen*
*Framed each disastrous scene*
*Over and over and over again*
*As if looking for some mean*
*And in passivity they watched*
*Drunk on the horror*
*Of the massive devastation*
*Looking like rapist in condemnation*
*Glaring upon their freshly used prey*
*They strutted their voices*
*And applauded their pictorial choices*
*As a nation splayed upon laid*
*For them – it was a wonderful day*

## Saprophyte

*Love not fully exposed to the sun*
*Retreats into shadows*
*Before the day is done*
*And has no where to go*
*And has no where to grow*
*And has no where*
*To run*

### The Real McGruder – Aaron

*Has drama been played out*
*In every imaginable scene and scheme*
*Until the imagination is exhausted*
*And the names change*
*Only to increase revenues?*
*For I can do what you can do*
*And just as insanely*
*And now the animals*
*Are just as smart as I*
*Except I don't climb trees anymore*
*Well except to get my cat*
*Who knew that I would come to get her*
*Have we exhausted everything?*
*Have we exhausted nature*
*Into global warming?*
*Have we exhausted love from*
*Its wonderful to its lurid forms*
*Sealing our eggs and sperm in test tubes*
*For rainy day genetic jugglers?*
*Have we exhausted reality*
*Except for the comics where Bin Laden*
*Finds his plots…*
*Kill the strips*

## *Home Coming*

*How did a world so round*
*Become so flat and square*
*We fought another war then found*
*Not a hint of weapons there*
*And now in peace we have lost*
*More soldiers than in war*
*To continue this course at any cost*
*Is more futile than before*

*Freedom now is wrapped in constriction*
*And to the very Right we've run*
*The boa's home land security interdiction*
*Observes and records everyone*
*While intentions are as shallow as mirrors*
*Bias and phobias once more set free*
*Imprisoned by our very fears*
*No freer now than our soldiers must be*

## *Mirrors*

*I have sat and listened to the sounds*
*Of the ghosts that inherit the winds*
*And heard their pain on sheets of echoes*
*Crying out in circular breaths*

*In a world of lesions*
*Booze and blow magnetize then cauterize*
*Noses throats and veins*
*Inducing them to scab*

*Once they were the rapid transit*
*Steaming down cerebral monorails*
*Drawn to the spikes*
*With the social mix devoted to the fix*

*I have watched their serpentine parades*
*And found my body hairs saluting*
*As they rolled into the shade*
*To germinate from a bottle or a vial*

*While the reaper sits at the throttle*
*To snare tormented minds*
*By sucking souls out of bodies in leaning and*
*Conducting their breaths through winter's reeds*

*I have sat and listened to the sounds*
*Of these ghosts that inherit the winds*
*I even placed my ear to the ground*
*To insure that I'm not them*

## Landers

*Landers was sacrificed today*
*Instead of being allowed to play*
*Not once in his deed did his dad understand*
*That the child he was beating was not the man*
*Who had caused him his fear or his frustration*
*But he drew on his pride from a bottle's damnation*
*And over and over his fist would fly*
*And he never saw himself in the corner of his eye*
*Or heard himself in the cries of his son*
*So he beat poor Landers till he thought he had won*
*This warped psychotic cyclic scheme*
*Manifested in nightmares and stolen dreams*
*Indelible black scars carved on ebony skin*
*Which dyed both the life and the love that got in*

## Twisted Tears

*Ragged old man rocking and reeking*
*Could you be the father I'm seeking*
*Or are you the one in the Armani suit*
*Who left after giving my mother some toot*

*Little old lady clinging to sanity*
*Exploring garbage spouting profanity*
*Now you've lost all your vanity*
*Another soul sacrificed for humanity*

*Shy little girl first day of school*
*Ninety degrees and you're wearing wool*
*Hard to keep your mind on your books*
*Don't have to turn to feel the looks*

*Crippled kid with the name of Dennis*
*Unable to play football or tennis*
*Tells jokes trying to win us*
*We laugh but is there decency within us*

*Octogenarian looking at walls*
*Wondering about times we recall*
*Life exists from visit to visit*
*Other than that he just sits and fidgets*

*Running scared looking for love*
*Searching for someone just to hug*
*Love in its platonic form*
*I've got AIDS and now you're gone*

*No wonder*
*Time just slips right on away*

# *The Temptation Walk*

*Anger and violence*
*And what to do with it*
*Glocks bring silence*
*Short life and then you're through it*
*Caught up in the mind games*
*Another bullet to the brain*
*When it's over who remains*
*Just those who were to blame*
*And members of the decease*
*Are ready to disturb the peace*
*And take out to the streets*
*Committing drive-bys for release*
*"Like a snowball rolling down the side*
*of a snow covered hill…"*

# *Slipping the Bonds*

*No one knows the trouble I've seen*
*It's been stopped up in my head*
*And never disappears at night*
*Not even when I'm in bed*

*With eyes wide shut or open real tight*
*It's the same trouble night or day*
*It gnaws at my body and soul*
*Eroding them both away*

*I've cried out loud in my smallest voice*
*I tried to chase trouble away*
*But now I'm left with just one choice*
*I'll strangle it today*

*Here is all the strength I've got*
*I wish I had much more*
*I'll set a noose about trouble's neck*
*With a slip knot on the door*

*It's strange to see me dangling beside him*
*About two feet off the floor*
*But I am free of this asylum*
*For trouble has hands no more*

# Wisdom

**Spoons for the placid**
**Forks for the divergent trails**
**Knives for the slayers**

## *Sky Writing*

*I gave my heart flight*
        *And left its truths*
                *Like vapor trails*
                *On jet streams*

*For you to face*
        *AND*
*For you to trace*

*To entice your heart*
        *To grow and rise*
        *OR*
        *Ground us here and now*
                *As crippled*

                        *As we are*

# *Graffiti*

*Sprayed and splayed*
*In aerosols of*
*Reds and blues*
*White and pinks*
*On sidewalks*
*Underpasses and over walls*
*In stagnant alley ways*
*While other canvases trundle*
*Down tracks*
*Leaving for anywhere*
*Heading toward somewhere*
*Carrying cries*
*Coated and coded*
*On sleek silvers*
*Or rusted reds*
*A Picasso's still life*
*For all to view*
*But few to understand*

## *NO*

*Our breathing discovered patterns*
*And swirled us into sheets*
*Like hot wax around a candle*
*Images were projected on to walls*
*As our love grew*
*Slowly a "No"*
*Was blown into my ear*
*Teasing tickling tantalizing*
*As if to intensify this moment*
*Your half closed eyes*
*And the quivering in your smile*
*Requested my confidence*
*And so a kiss was formed*
*And our fingers traced geographies*
*Stirring the flames within us*

*In love's mid harvest*
*Perfumed moisture glistened upon your breast*
*Your nipples grew as erect as the island's palms*
*My moist lips and yours*
*Poised pursed and pulsating*
*Our bodies found their natural rhythms*
*And as we ventured on*
*"No" again breeched the silence*
*That only lovers know*

*That point in time where gravity frees flight*
*Where purpose finds its destination*
*Where trust bridges the river of fear*
*And creates unity*
*But "No" had disturbed the guards*
*Who now stood as firm*
*As I had been*

*Faced with this life's incongruity*
*The pain and all its cruelty*
*Should I be singed by mind over matter*
*Or incinerated by just the reverse?*

*"!?NO?!"*

## Linen

*Linen like silk*
*Woven by the orient*
*Once frivolous incantations*
*Captured the hearts of nations*
*Half of a living octagon*
*All swelled with song*

*None of us were without tune*
*Gals and lads alike*
*Worlds upon worlds were totally swooned*
*Then linen cut the mic*
*There sat a world less moon*
*Left to a lonely knight*

*Linen worn many times*
*May deeply wrinkle and fray*
*Borne by hidden stresses*
*Which were veiled in the parade*
*We were drawn by his charisma*
*But he couldn't get away*

*Linen like silk*
*Woven by the orient*
*Knew that life was heaven sent*
*And knew what love really meant*
*Devoted until the final rent*
*Left this world in discontent*
*With his notes pressed to our hearts*

## How Did You Know

*How did we grow*
*From swinging on swings*
*To hugging and kissing*
*And other things?*
*I still sit in awe*
*Of all that I saw*
*But how did you know?*

*How did you know*
*From first touch of our fingers*
*Magic was there and always would linger?*
*Until today it was hidden away in my mind*
*I was so blind*
*But*
*How did you know?*

*Now that I'm here*
*So close to you*
*How does the night*
*Know the moon's exact view?*
*To loose your splendor*
*And warmth of your skin*
*When sheets enfold you*
*And I'm there within*

*I could sit*
*And watch you breathe*
*For as long as it takes*
*An atheist to believe*
*How did you know*
*That this could only grow?*
*Honey I'm sure now*
*But before now*
*How did you know?*

## *September Love*

*Tender do I love this time*
*Remembering*
*How hard it fell upon me*
*Daze gone by*
*Until I recalled*
*The wall that I had met*
*And wept*
*By the stones*
*That held their ground*
*While I dissolved*

*Crimson eyes ran redder*
*Abraded by brash winds*
*Whose criticisms*
*Left whelps upon my skin*
*Which clothes could not conceal*
*Receipts of a first love*
*Whose price was*
*To lay the lash*
*On a virgin heart*
*And then to watch me bleed*

*Funny*
*How wounds heal with scars*
*And hearts with memories*
*Which come and go*
*Fast or slow*
*Like the leaves upon the trees*
*Whose branches remain*
*To welcome them again*
*In the spring*
*When love is king*

*Tender do I love this time*
*Not for revenge or revenue*
*Not even for sovereignty*
*But with this heart*
*Whose soul's intent*
*Wishes only for us*
*To break soil and breathe*
*And I will rush solely*
*To insure that you my love*
*Are inebriated with life*
*But never to rush our harvest...*

## *The Theft*

*Love has wrenched itself from life*
*And hidden beneath some jagged cold stones*
*Futility's search on moonless nights*
*Or days of eclipse – yet the search goes on*

*Nothing seems to stunt my memory*
*Though time may alter its symmetry*
*And you are summoned back to me*
*But never again in reality*

*And so I savor this emanation*
*Whose presence now is a present for me*
*And set once more our lives in motion*
*With the wrapping once more set out to sea*

*Love surfaces from these depths*
*And is just as real as I am swept*
*Once more to the shore where secrets were kept*
*Once more to love's bed where we slept*

*Time resumes in early mourning*
*For now my senses return to me*
*You left, my love, without enough warning*
*And with out you what can life be?*

## *Peace*

*Drawn by flowers and morning dew*
*With fragrances that mesmerize too*
*A sun reflected crystalline glen*
*Allowed me to view its discipline*
*And hoped in time that I'd forget*
*In fact it may have held its breath*

*Delicate wings graced butterflies*
*That in this valley filled the skies*
*With so many colors and so little room*
*The flowers were forbidden to show their blooms*
*These ballerinas in disguise*
*Did pirouettes on the petals' limbs*
*Collecting nectar as their prize*
*At least until the sunlight dimmed*

*Upon its floor I did lay*
*To view the magic it displayed*
*The stars came out and filled the skies*
*While those that fell formed fireflies*
*They glowed like fragments of the sun*
*And blended faintly as the dawn did come*
*Sweet morning glories then filled the air*
*And comforts now – when I'm in despair*
*With scenes like this it isn't hard*
*To see and feel and be touched by God*

## *The Conscience of Purgatory*

*is the conscience a barnacle*
*on life's hull*
*that increases the coefficient of drag*

*which causes mine to lag*
*problems created but not solved*
*often accused but seldom absolved*

*if waters flood these corners*
*and use my cheeks for spillways*
*where can i go*

*do you know*
*if closet doors are secure enough to*
*keep the skeletons at bay*

*or can i rely on tears*
*to cleanse all of yesterdays sins*
*and wash tomorrows away*

*if solutions are like the face of glass*
*why do i hesitate when faced with a mirror*
*or will i be purged at last*

# Free-Dam

*Nikki*
*Ebony scarlet & jade*
*Are the threads you saved*
*And wove Into America's Quilt*
*Identifying the cause*
*Discovering the guilt*
*Expressing the inequities,*
*Demanding the justice*
*Delving into Human rights*
*You pinched, pierced then*
*Touched U.S.*
*(Both Cerebrum and integument)*
*How can we now*
*Seem so content*

*Shredded threads now*
*Blunt the brains and sever the voices*
*Dubbing us rainbow mutes*
*Scarlet ribbons bleed*
*As the processions of*
*Anemic choices intercede while*
*Echoes of wails and groans*
*From the very tapestry*
*Of ebony sunburned*
*backs bent in morns*
*And shackled in seas of jade*
*Whose faces would never see the sun but*
*Whose hopes would never fade yet*
*Whose victory was never won*
*We must not remain suspended*
*Hanged in effigy*
*By a type of stereo still unending*
*That never sets us free*
*And only yields strange fruit*

## *Winter*

*Whirling winds*
*Overcoats and mittens*
*Fireplaces and cuddling kittens*
*Skeletal trees*
*And quilted grounds*
*Crunching footsteps*
*Interrupt sounds*
*Of snowflakes*
*Falling on the floor*
*When kissed by sunlight*
*Gone once more*
*Whirling winds then declare*
*Though presently slumbering*
*Spring is near*

# *Ashes From Other Loves*

*Captive in sunlight*
*Ruby lips and rounded hips*
*Imprison by night*

# *The Blossom's Fruit*

*If love were satiety*
*And solely made in bed*
*Then bodies and souls*
*Always would be fed*
*And never would we ever*
*Have to lift our heads*
*Or open our minds*
*To its hunger*

# The Primrose Pyre

*Nearing a fire just to keep warm*
*Cautiously I ventured*
*To keep myself from harm*
*But enchanted by the flame*
*And in its comfort I became*
*An unwilling victim to its pain*

*With wings singed and flight now lost*
*Me – the self imprisoned moth*
*Trapped in a one man holocaust*
*I became chilled by the very thought*
*Of all the damages it has wrought*
*Again and again and again*

*Tonight the peacock*
*But are you willing to hear*
*His singing mornings*

# *In Sync*

*She forever thought of him*
*From sunup until the daylight dimmed*
*Her heart had held such intensity*
*His too felt this immensity*
*But only at a moment's whim*

*So she gave all of her heart*
*And found that he wanted only a part*
*In one moment she felt so complete*
*In the next—stained—unable to speak*
*She knew she hadn't been that smart*

*Love for some means all your life*
*Love for others – but a moment*
*Love's timing should be more precise*
*Or perhaps forever remain dormant*

## When Ron Smiles

*Remove the cinders*
*Gathered by evening*
*While the sun*
*Dissolves crystals*
*That littered the lawns*
*Listen to the chirping*
*Pierce the day's silence*
*It's time for the living*
*To sing life's song*

*For those of you*
*Who stayed in bed*
*Or had another*
*Appointment ahead*
*We carry your love*
*And this burden instead*
*Of lowering our heads*
*To concede*
*That you're gone*

*How do the living*
*Take life for granted*
*Surely it's slanted*
*Not held but seeps through*
*I can't imagine what life*
*Would have meant*
*Could have been spent*
*Without that smile too*
*Within us you'll always live on*

*As long as I exist there's a part of Ron that I will miss*
*And the rest...*
*I will always carry with me*

## JUDY Judy judy

Love unrequited
Extremely short sighted
Lends its lap
And arms
To comfort and caress
The chilling drafts
Captured in half closed doorways

Memories of affection
Opaque crystalline illusions
Trapped in gray time capsules
And dangled from the
Slender precipice of reality
Entrusted to support
An entire galaxy

If spring is winter's residue
Then ashes of this love
Should serve to
Cure pain and
Cleanse the cracked glass
Restoring vision to view
Eyesores from the past

How long will I remain
Cast in this shadow's storm
That only fools retain
Guarding and keeping you from harm
And holding on
To a heart most dear
That dissolved so long ago

## *Columbust*

No winds will beckon
As peril lies but a footstep away
Nor will words find a voice
For this and other yesterdays
When they were the shards that cut and bruised
Now silence explores the wounds' excuses
Compounded by calm's abuses

When did this residence begin
We could only have hosted this siege
Pent up by walls that grew higher
While isolating us was Pavlov's wire
Permitting egos to further erect
Misfortunes that even strangers detect
Flaws splayed out on floors

Time was once a consideration
Now a condition of incarceration
Arid as the Sahara
Forever in drought
Not even a tear to birth
Or cleanse a thought
Incurable damages that the distance has wrought

Muffled phone conversations
Behind closed doors hold more
Than drafts and speculation
While impaled upon pins and nails
Hearts have lost all of their sensations
And I am left with the realization
That on the morrow I sail

## Echoes from the Caverns in my Mind

*I yearn for spring*
*Warm sunny glorious days*
*Royal blue skies*
*Candy cotton clouds*
*Diamond studded morning dew*
*Sprinklers*
*Chirping robins*
*Barking dogs*
*Ice cream trucks*
*Warm breezes*
*Lying down in grass*
*Tulips and roses*
*Shorts and t-shirts*
*Flip flops and sandals*
*Lovers holding hands*
*Beaches and bikinis*
*Sunglasses and tanning lotion*
*Rafts and radios*
*Skinny dipping*
*Marco Polo and volleyball*
*Picnics and kites*
*Motor boats and skiing*
*Bicycles and skateboards*
*Monkey bars and sand boxes*
*See saws and swings*
*Zoos and amusement parks*
*Hide-n-seek and hop scotch*
　*And children laughing*
　　*And children playing*
　　　*And children laughing*
　　　　*And children playing*
　　　　　*And children laughing*
　　　　　　*And children playing…*

## Within a Heart Beat's Interval
### 11/18/29 "Honey" 11/22/04

*Roll the drum slowly*
*Hold fast fleeting sun*
*For yesterday's assurances*
*Today have reaped*
*The cruelty of fear and phobias*
*In as much as reasons foundation*
*Has been disfigured*
*Then this season deserves*
*No celebrity*

*Hollow out this day*
*Turn its rind inside out*
*Let this eclipse endure*
*Or may I forfeit my heart*
*Drop it here and now*
*For this burden is far too great*
*And while possessing it*
*Leaves me without the strength to move*
*And with even less to beg*

*Roll the drum slowly*
*That each note's interval*
*Might serve to strengthen my grasp*
*And from this rung retrieve you back*
*To this day to this time and to this love*
*Life's logic now disowns me*
*For it was you who*
*Gave life more*
*Than voice or song*

*You were the lion's heart and ferocity*
*You were her tenacity*
*The pride's alpha*
*And its longevity*
*Suspend this time that*
*Life in retrospect may weigh*
*Its misappropriated lifespan of a butterfly*
*Whose tactile and vocal touches*
*Were once staples of Honey now vanished*

*Roll the drum slowly now*
*That I may reconsider the depth of her prosperity*
*For even angels with dented halos*
*Bless and infect us with their integrity*
*And infuse commitment and patience*
*As they display and define love*
*With such a deft touch*
*Even rocks may absorb the tears from her labors*
*And blossom into souls…*

## *At Last*

*It's been a while*
*Since we've sat*
*And sat*
*Yes, I've missed that*
*It's been a while*

*It's been a while*
*Since we took a walk*
*Or talked and talked*
*Of things we've thought*
*It's been a while*

*It's been a while*
*Since I've seen your smile*
*That captured laughs*
*That lasted for miles*
*It's been a while*

*It's been a while*
*Since we touched hands*
*That conformed to demands*
*But then had other plans*
*It's been a while*

*It's been a while*
*Since the winter's snow*
*Yet how could we know*
*That our hearts melt so slow*
*It's been a while*

*It's been a while*
*Since my last request*
*That you return my happiness*
*And if ever I've been blessed*
*It's been a while*

*May age grant you wisdom*
*And may wisdom bring you the gift of love*
*The ability to Know when it is real*
*And the Good sense*
*To hold on to it once found*

*If love's presiding light is longevity*
*This now is just*
*The dawn...*

**Thalamus' Ink.**

LaVergne, TN USA
10 March 2010
175595LV00003B/2/A